Pebble Plus

T0069582

Investigate the Seasons

Let's Look at Fall

Revised Edition

by Sarah L. Schuette

CAPSTONE PRESS
a capstone imprint

Pebble Plus is published by Capstone Press,
1710 Roe Crest Drive, North Mankato, Minnesota 56003
www.capstonepub.com

Copyright © 2018 by Capstone Press, a Capstone imprint.
All rights reserved. No part of this publication may be reproduced in whole or in part, or stored in a retrieval system, or transmitted in any form or by any means, electronic, mechanical, photocopying, recording, or otherwise, without written permission of the publisher

Library of Congress Cataloging-in-Publication Data
is available on the Library of Congress website.

ISBN 978-1-5435-0860-4 (library binding)
ISBN 978-1-5435-0876-5 (paperback)
ISBN 978-1-5435-0880-2 (ebook pdf)

Editorial Credits
Sarah Bennett, designer; Tracy Cummins, media researcher, Laura Manthe, production specialist

Photo Credits
Shutterstock: Dave Allen Photography, 7, DmZ, 5, Erik Mandre, 15, FotoRequest, 13, Grisha Bruev, 9, images72, 17, Liubou Yasiukovich, Cover Design Element, Manamana, 11, Nancy Gill, 19, nikitsin.smugmug.com, 1, Piotr Krzeslak, Cover, Sofiaworld, 3, Victor Grow, 21

Note to Parents and Teachers

The Investigate the Seasons set supports national science standards related to weather and life science. This book describes and illustrates the season of fall. The images support early readers in understanding the text. The repetition of words and phrases helps early readers learn new words. This book also introduces early readers to subject-specific vocabulary words, which are defined in the Glossary section. Early readers may need assistance to read some words and to use the Table of Contents, Glossary, Read More, Internet Sites, Critical Thinking Questions, and Index sections of the book.

Printed in the United States 6073

Table of Contents

It's Fall! 4

Animals in Fall 10

Plants in Fall 16

What's Next? 20

Glossary 22

Read More 23

Internet Sites 23

Critical Thinking Questions 24

Index 24

It's Fall!

How do you know it's fall?

A cool breeze blows.

The weather is colder.

Leaves change color.

They flutter to the ground.

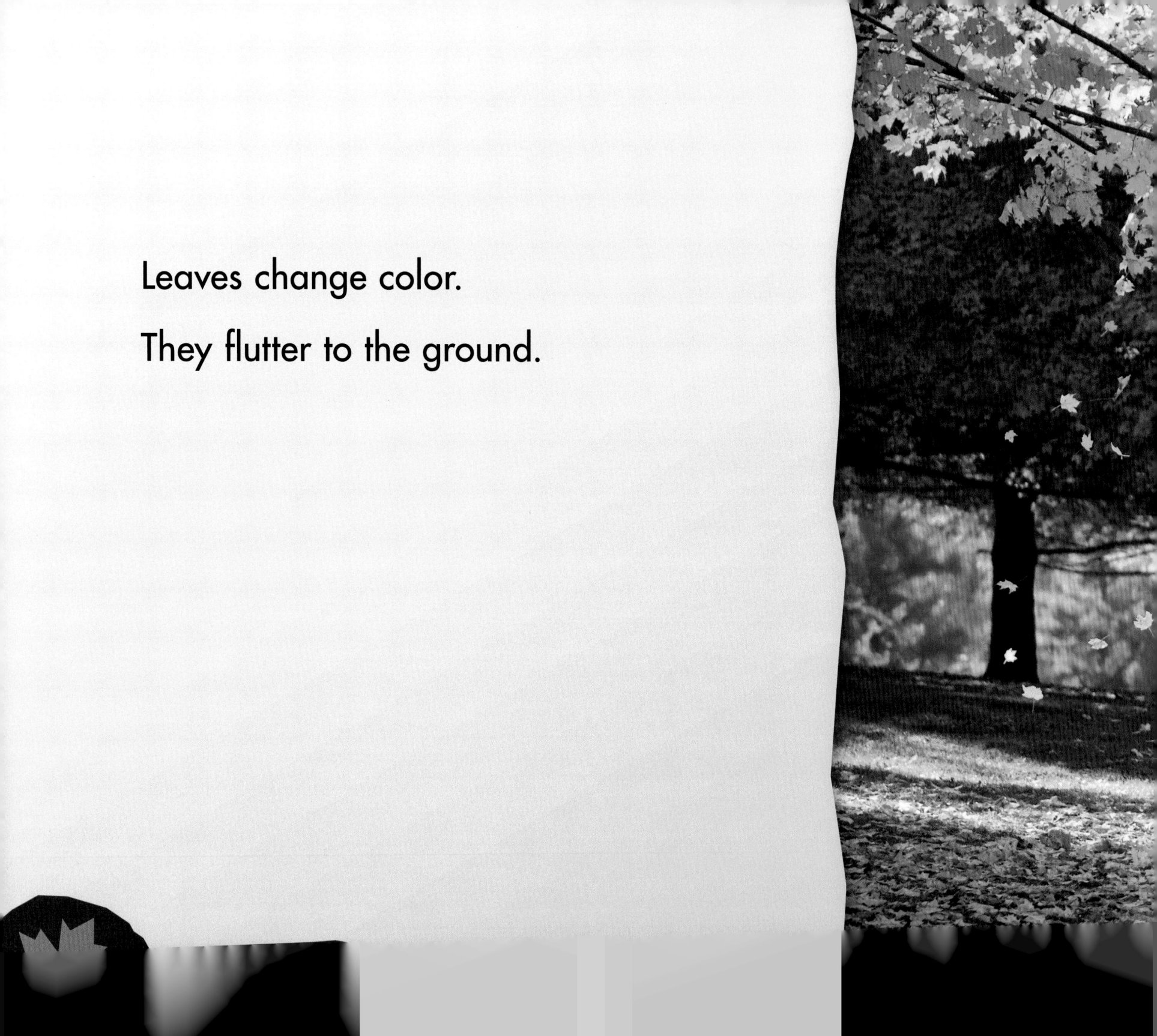

The sun sets earlier.
Fall days are shorter
than summer days.

Animals in Fall

What do animals do in fall?

Squirrels rush around.

They gather nuts

to store for winter.

Birds fly south.

They look

for warmer weather.

Bears search for a place

to hibernate.

Their fur coats grow thicker.

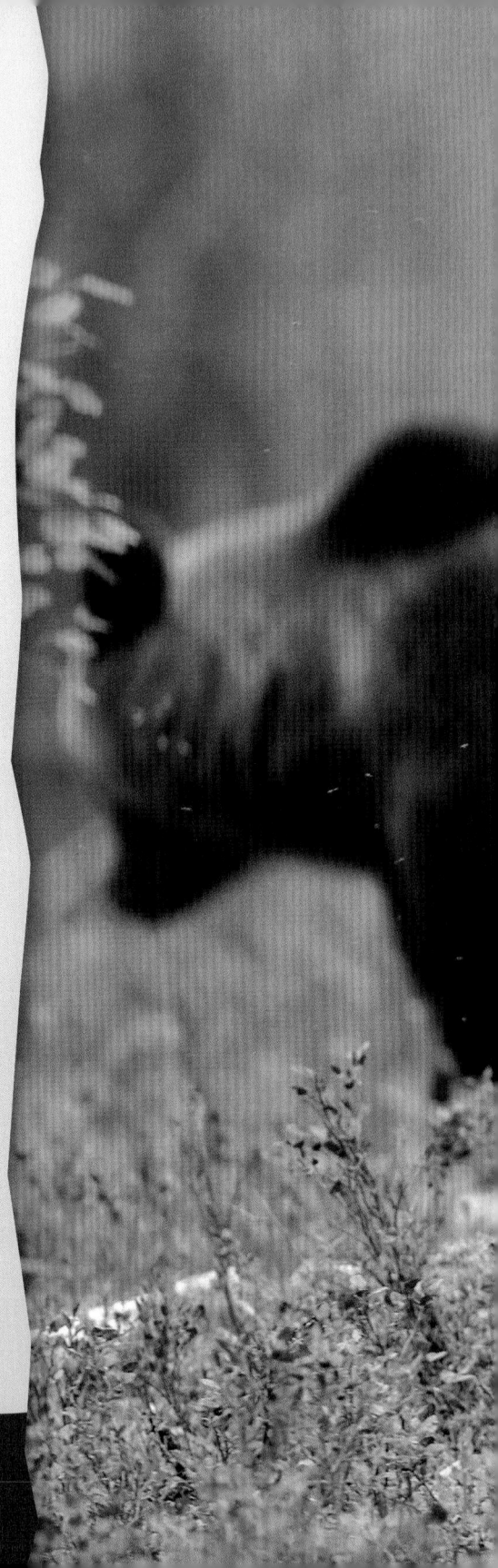

Plants in Fall

What happens
to plants in fall?
Ripe apples fill the orchard.
They're ready to be picked.

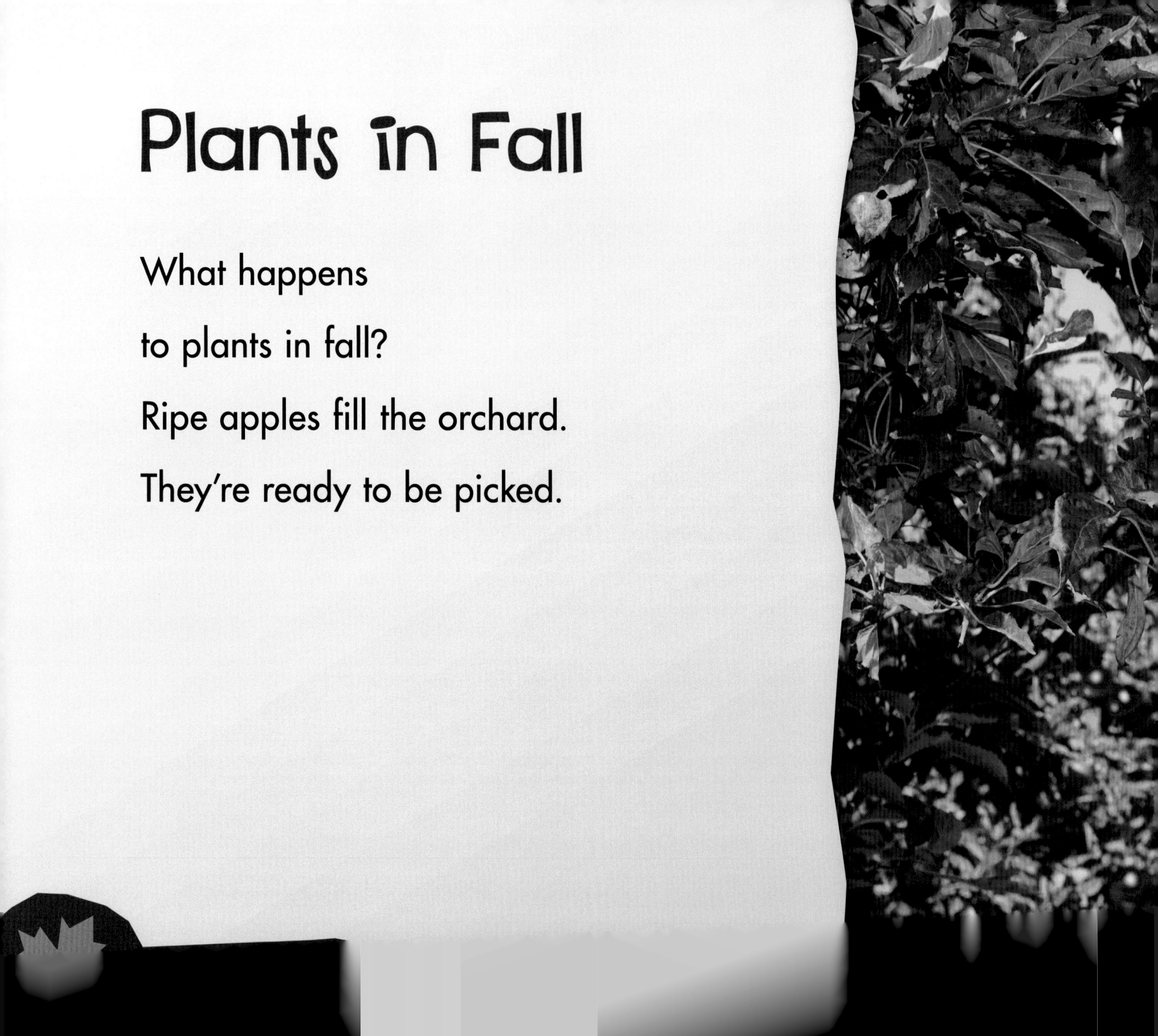

Corn ripens in the field.

It's ready to be harvested.

What's Next?

The temperature grows cold.

Fall is over.

What season is next?

Glossary

breeze—a gentle wind

flutter—to wave, flap, or float in a breeze; leaves flutter as they drop off tree branches

harvest—to gather crops that are ready to be picked; fall is a time for harvesting crops such as corn, soybeans, wheat, and oats

hibernate—to spend the winter in a deep sleep

orchard—a field or farm where fruit trees grow

ripen—to become ready to be picked

season—one of the four parts of the year; winter, spring, summer, and fall are seasons

weather—the condition outdoors at a certain time and place; weather changes with each season

Read More

Appleby, Alex. *What Happens in Fall?* Four Super Seasons. New York: Gareth Stevens Pub., 2014.

Brennan, Linda Crotta. *Leaves Change Color.* Tell Me Why. Ann Arbor, Mich.: Cherry Lake Publishing, 2015.

Herrington, Lisa M. *How Do You Know it's Fall?* Rookie Read-About Science. New York: Children's Press, 2014.

Internet Sites

Use FactHound to find Internet sites related to this book.

Visit *www.facthound.com*

Just type 9781543508604 and go.

Critical Thinking Questions

1. Describe two signs that it is fall.

2. What do squirrels do in fall?

3. Describe what "harvest" means. Use the glossary to help you.

Index

animals, 10, 12, 14
apples, 16
bears, 14
birds, 12
breeze, 4
cold, 4, 20
corn, 18
fur, 14
harvesting, 16, 18
hibernating, 14
leaves, 6
nuts, 10
orchards, 16
plants, 16, 18
ripe, 16, 18
sun, 8
temperature, 4, 12, 20
weather, 4, 12